MY SiDEWALKS ON
SCOTT FORESMAN
READING STREET

# Communities

## Program Authors

Connie Juel, Ph.D.

Jeanne R. Paratore, Ed.D.

Deborah Simmons, Ph.D.

Sharon Vaughn, Ph.D.

Glenview, Illinois
Boston, Massachusetts
Chandler, Arizona
Hoboken, New Jersey

ISBN-13: 978-0-328-45270-5
ISBN-10:     0-328-45270-X

PEARSON

16  16

# Communities

# People in Communities

MY SiDEWALKS ON
SCOTT FORESMAN
READING STREET

# Communities in Nature

# Contents

# Families Together

**See page 31 for My New Words and Pictionary!**

# Families Together

Mom, Dad, and Fran plan a fun trip.

Look at my map, Mom and Dad.
We can go here.

Drip, drip, drip.

Rub the pot, Pam.
Rub the lid, Fred.

Skip can run to Dad.
Skip can run to Stan.

Run, Skip, run!
It is fun!

# Circus Families

by Fred Roberts • illustrated by Peter Grosshauser

See the fun in the tent.

They skip and flip.
They bump and slip.

Brent and Pam flip flop on a mat.

Dad can flip, flip, flip.
Mom can flip and stand on top.

Blast can run to Mom and Kim.

Blast can hop up and spin fast.
Blast can spin like Mom and Kim.

Mom and Dad stand on stilts.

Pip must look up at Mom and Dad.
Pip has a red hat and a red belt.

Look at Mom go up to Sam.
Here is my hand, Sam.

It is fun in the tent!
Clap, clap, clap!

# Pests
## in the Garden

by Susan Adams

illustrated by Aleksey and Olga Ivanov

Look at the birds in the garden.

Birds can not help us here.

Mom, Dad, and Gus get rid of birds.

Mom got a big red dress.
Dad got a tan belt.

Mom and Gus can stuff it.
Dad can bend it up.

Gus got a big hat to add.

My big, big hat can sit on top.

Mom and Dad grin at Gus.
We can set it here, Gus.

Flap, flap, flap.
The big birds left the garden.

# Ants on a Log

Read Together

If you like peanut butter, here is a snack that you and your family can make together!

**Ingredients**

celery sticks

peanut butter

raisins

1. Wash and dry the celery sticks.

2. Spread peanut butter on the sticks.

3. Drop a few raisins on each peanut butter-filled log. Press gently.

4. Happy Eating!

Why do you think this snack is called Ants on a Log?

# My New Words

**here***       **Here** means at this place.
            We will stop **here**.

**my***         I forgot **my** gloves.

**to***          Are you going **to** the park?

*tested high-frequency words

# Pictionary

garden

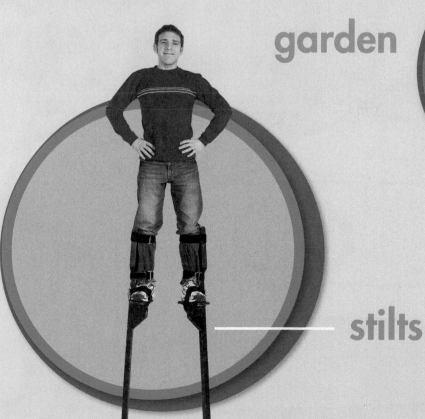

_____ stilts

# Contents

# School Days

See page 57 for My New Words and Pictionary!

3

Nan will help Ken fill the last spot.
But will it fit?

Snap! It is a snug fit.

Tad and Pam can spell.

They can print well.
*See the wig on the pig.*

Clint, Meg, and Dan are in a lab.
They spot a red crab.

Dan will print a fact on the pad.

One, two, three—step, step, step.
Gus and Nell twist and spin.

Twist and spin! Twist and spin!
They will not miss a step.

# Schools Around the World

by Rose Dell

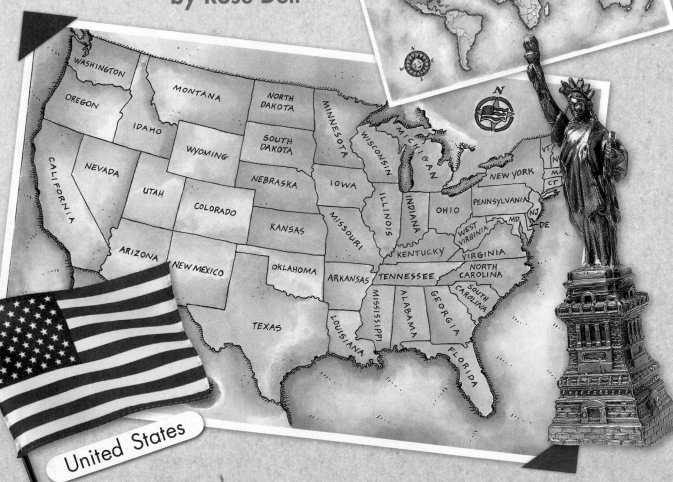

United States

Look at the flag and map.
You are here.

But get set.
We will go on a class trip!

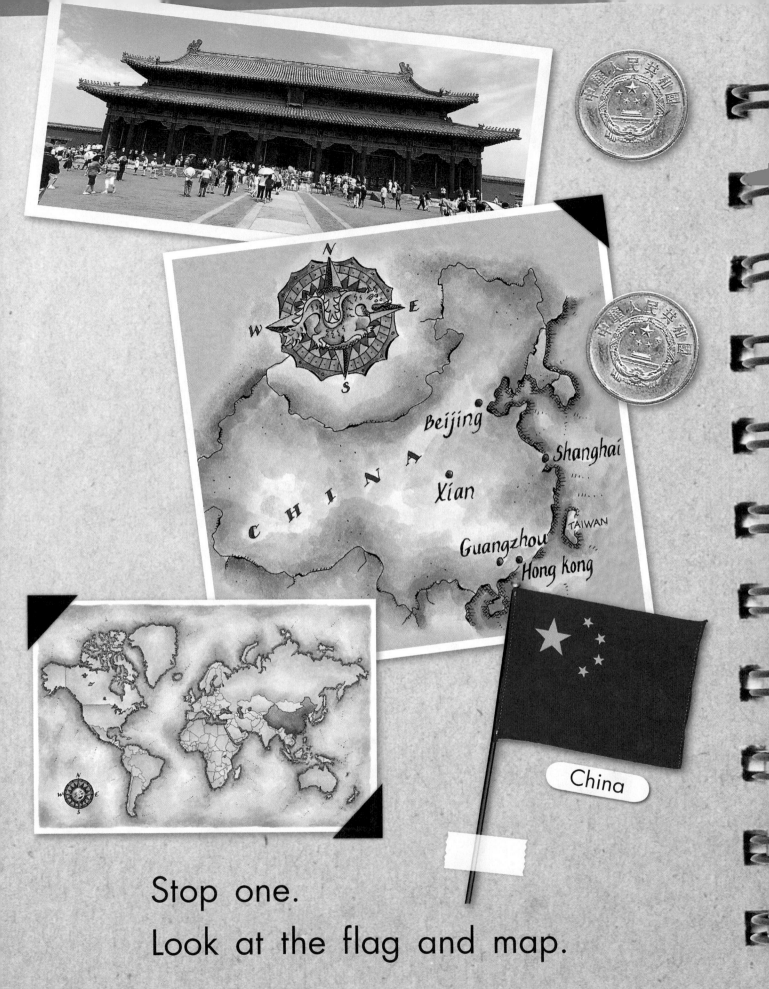

Stop one.
Look at the flag and map.

Jin will stand and tell a fact.
The rest will sit still—and not nap!

Stop two.
Look at the flag and map.

Pum! Pum! Men will hit the drum.
The class will clap, stomp, and hum.

Brazil

AMAZON RIVER

Fortaleza

BRAZIL

Salvador

Brasília

Rio de Janeiro

São

Pôrto

Stop three—last stop.
Look at the flag and map.

Sit up! Stand up! Jump! Jog! Skip!
The class will get fit.

# Max and Rex

by Josie West

illustrated by Anne Kennedy

Max is my best pal.

Rex is my best pal.

Rex has a big box.

Max can help Rex fix the box.

Max has a sax.
Just look at Max blast the sax.

Max can add well.
One plus two is three.

Rex can spell and print well.
Rex can help Max.

Max and Rex grin.

It is fun to have a best pal in class.

# Welcome to Our Classroom

**Sing Together**

(Sing to the tune of "Sing a Song of Sixpence.")

Welcome to our classroom.
Come in and sit right down.
We are all together.
Take a look around.

Here inside our classroom,
There's lots to see and do.
I am happy being here
And making friends with you!

# My New Words

**one***   **One** is the word for 1.
　　　　 **One** is also a single thing.

**three***   **Three** is the word for 3.
　　　　 **Three** is one more than two.

**two***   **Two** is the word for 2.
　　　　 **Two** is one more than one.

*tested high-frequency words

# Pictionary

flag

print ——

# Contents

58

# Our Neighbors

See page 83 for My New Words and Pictionary!

# Let's Find Out
# Our Neighbors

Val has a job on a big bus.

The big bus will stop at ten.
"Step up," said Val.

Ted has a hat and vest you can see.
Ted will help us.

Ted must stop the van.

Glen has a fun job.

He can help me.

Glen will get *Cat Facts* from the top.

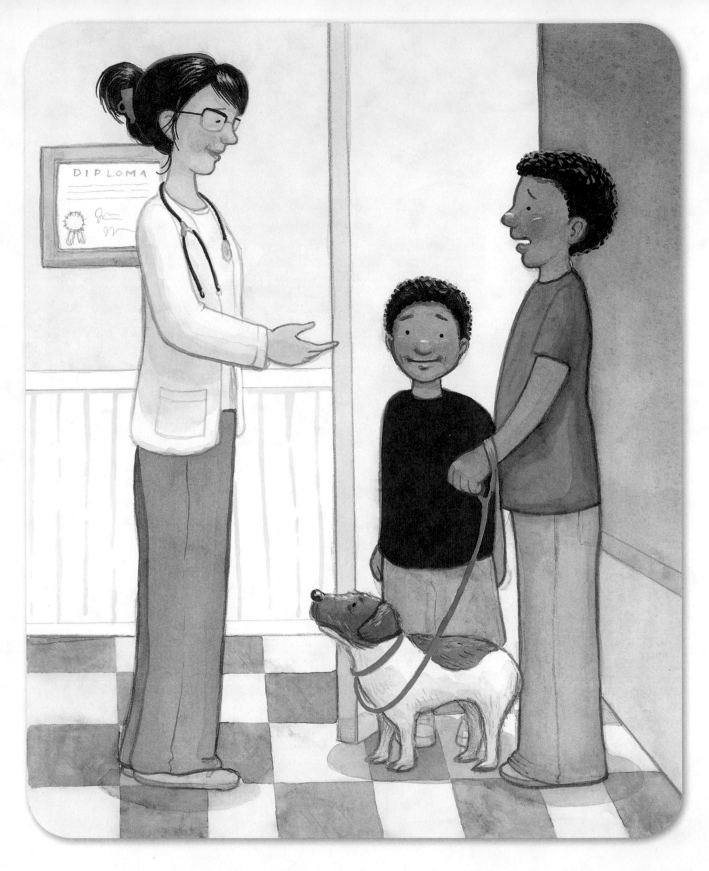

Viv is a vet.

My dog Skip is not well.

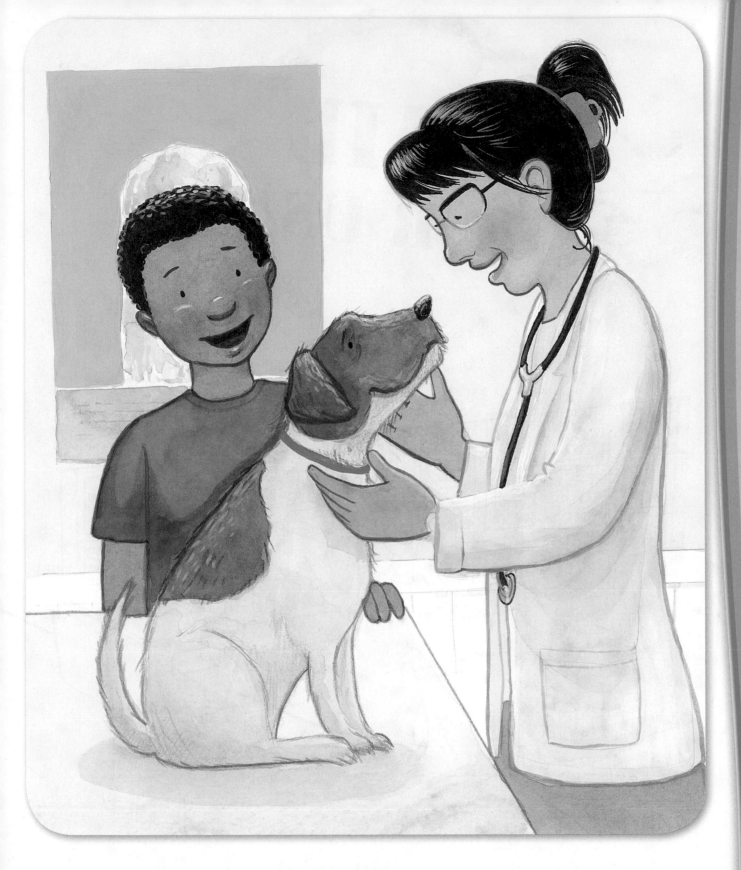

Viv can help Skip.

"I will fix up Skip," said Viv.

# MAIL FOR US

by Joyce Hamilton • illustrated by Sue Miller

Zaf will slip mail in the box.
It is a big job.

Next, Zaf must stuff mail in a bin.
Zaf will fill it up.

Get a vest and zip up, Zaf!
Zaf lifts the big bag.

Zaf will drop mail in the slot.
She must not stop. Zaf is fast.

Zaf will hand a box to Vik, the vet.
Vik is glad.

It is a disk.
It is a jazz disk!

"It is from my pen pal," said Max.
"Kim sent it to me."

Zaf and Max grin.

# New Neighbors

by Mandy Smith
illustrated by Victor Baldescu

Vin, Nell, and Pam just got here.
They have lots and lots to do.

Will they like it here?
Yes. Bev, Buzz, and Sam will help.

"Here is a pot of yams," said Bev.
Vin, Nell, and Pam like yams!

Vin and Buzz look at a bad vent.
"I can help you fix it," said Buzz.

Sam and Rex see Pam and Zip.
"Is Rex fast? Zip is," said Pam.

Sam and Pam run. Rex and Zip run.
Yip! Yip! Yap! Yap!

# Riddle Time

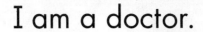

I am a doctor.
I make pets better.
Sometimes I give them shots.
Who am I?

I help keep you safe.
I have a special badge.
My car has lights on top.
Who am I?

I have lots of books around me.
I can help you read.
I work in a quiet place.
Who am I?

Answers: vet; police officer; librarian

82

# My New Words

**from***     Steel is made **from** iron.

**me***     Please give **me** a piece of paper.

**said***     She **said** she would help us.

*tested high-frequency words

# Pictionary

mail

disk

# Contents

We like to work together.

# Animals
## Working Together

See page 109 for My New Words and Pictionary!

# Animals Working Together

"Yip! Yip! Yip!"
The pup was mad.

Mom will help the pup.
Dad will hunt for Mom and his pup.

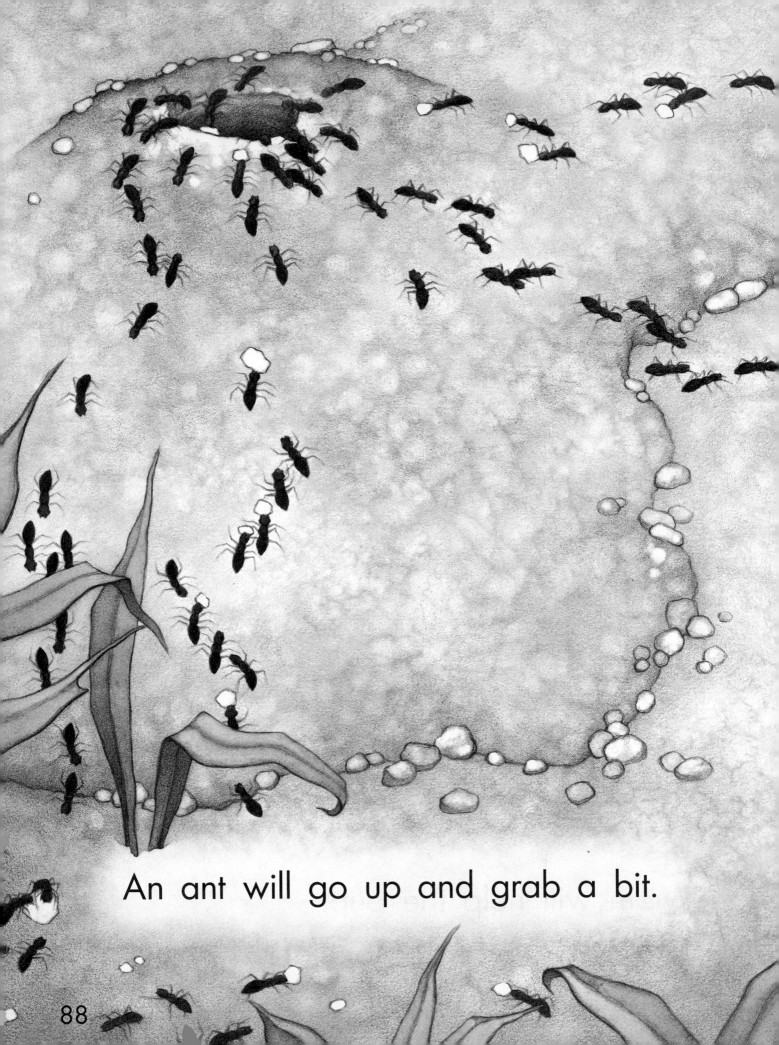

An ant will go up and grab a bit.

An ant will go to the nest.
It will not stop. It will not quit.

What is it?
It is a pod.

The pod will swim fast.
The pod will hunt.

# Lions Together

by Jonathan Champlin

Mom, Dad, and Cub are in a pride.
Mom and Dad can rest on grass.

Cub can jump and jab and run.
Cub can nap.

The pride can help Cub.
Mom can lick Cub.

Cub will look for Mom to get milk.

Quick! Quick! Run fast and hunt.
What luck will they have?

The hunt was the best!
It fed Mom, Dad, and Cub.

# Busy Beavers

by Quinn Mann

illustrated by Jackie Stafford

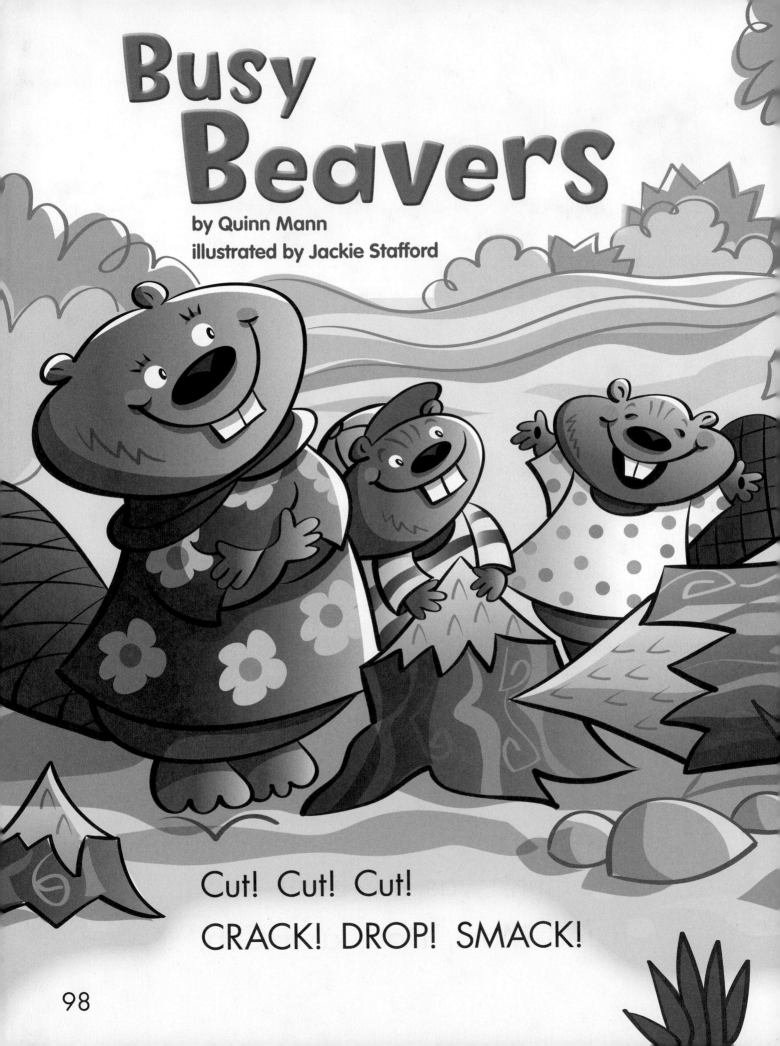

Cut! Cut! Cut!
CRACK! DROP! SMACK!

"It was a snap!" said Dad.

"Jack will cut big sticks," said Mom.
"Mack will pick up sticks and twigs."

"Drag sticks and twigs to the pond.
Sticks and twigs are for the dam."

Slap! Slap! Slap! "What is it?"

"It is Fox! It is Fox!" said Dad.
"Quick! Quick! Swim fast."

"Fox went back to his den.
What luck!" said Dad.

"Pack mud on the sticks and twigs."

The dam is as snug as a bug
in a rug.

Mom and Dad can rest on the dam.
Jack and Mack can sit and snack.

# Pods and Prides and Herds, Oh My!

## What do you call these groups of animals?

school of fish

gaggle of geese

herd of buffalo

pod of whales

charm of hummingbirds

pride of lions

# My New Words

**for***      Dad gave me money **for** lunch.

**was***      He **was** very shy.

**what***      **What** did you say? I don't know **what** she said.

*tested high-frequency words

# Pictionary

dam

pride

# Contents

# Plants and Animals

**See page 135 for My New Words and Pictionary!**

# Let's Find Out
# Plants and Animals

Can bugs help plants?
Yes! Yellow plant bits stick on bugs.

Look at bits drop from bugs to buds.
What pops from buds?

Can plants help bugs?

Yes! Bugs must have drops.
A bug sips plant drops.

Plants help bugs.
But can plants help birds?

116

Yes! A green bug rests on a plant.
The blue bird snacks on green bugs.

And can birds help plants?
Yes! The green bug is bad for plants.

Birds snack on bad bugs.
It helps plants.

# Plants Eat Bugs!

by Jill Ellison

Bugs can snack on plants.
But can plants snack on bugs?

The yellow plant has big cups.
A bug gets stuck in a big cup.

A black bug is resting.
It is on the green plant.

Snap! The quick plant traps the bug.
The plant is snacking on the bug!

A plant stands next to Big Blue Pond.
A bug is sticking on the plant.

The plant will snack on it.
Plants can snack on bugs. Yum! Yum!

# In the Sun

by Robert Dunn • illustrated by Cathy Shimmen

Sad Rex is hot, hot, hot!
What can block the sun for Rex?

Grass is blocking the sun for Ant.
Can Rex fit next to Ant? He can not.

Bob is a green and yellow bird.
Bob sits.

A blue plant is blocking the sun.
Can Rex fit next to Bob? He can not.

Bess is a big, tan dog.
Bess naps.

Big green twigs are blocking the sun.
Can Rex fit next to Bess? He can not.

"Plants help Ant, Bob, and Bess.
Can plants help me?" Rex asks.

Rex spots a big, big plant.
At last! It blocks the sun for Rex!

# Did You Know?

Elephants can eat up to 500 pounds of food in one day. That's a lot of food! Do you know what elephants eat?

Rabbits eat about a cup of vegetables a day. Do you know which vegetables rabbits like best?

Panda bears spend almost 16 hours a day eating. That's a long time! Do you know what pandas like to eat?

# My New Words

**blue***    **Blue** is the color of a clear sky during the day.

**green***    **Green** is the color of most growing plants.

**yellow***   **Yellow** is the color of lemons and butter.

*tested high-frequency words

# Pictionary

bird

twigs

# Contents

# Bugs
## Working Together

See page 159 for My New Words and Pictionary!

# Bugs
## Working Together

Bugs can work together.
Black ants can lift lots and lots.

And buzzing bugs can put stuff here.
Bugs can help bugs.

Can kids work together?
Yes. Kids can.

Kids can work like bugs.
Where? Come and see.

Kids lift lots and lots.
And kids can put stuff here.

Kids can help kids.
Bugs can help bugs.

# Home, Sweet Home

by José Galina ■ illustrated by Alan Baker

Black ants can dig big nests.
Ant nests can look like hills.

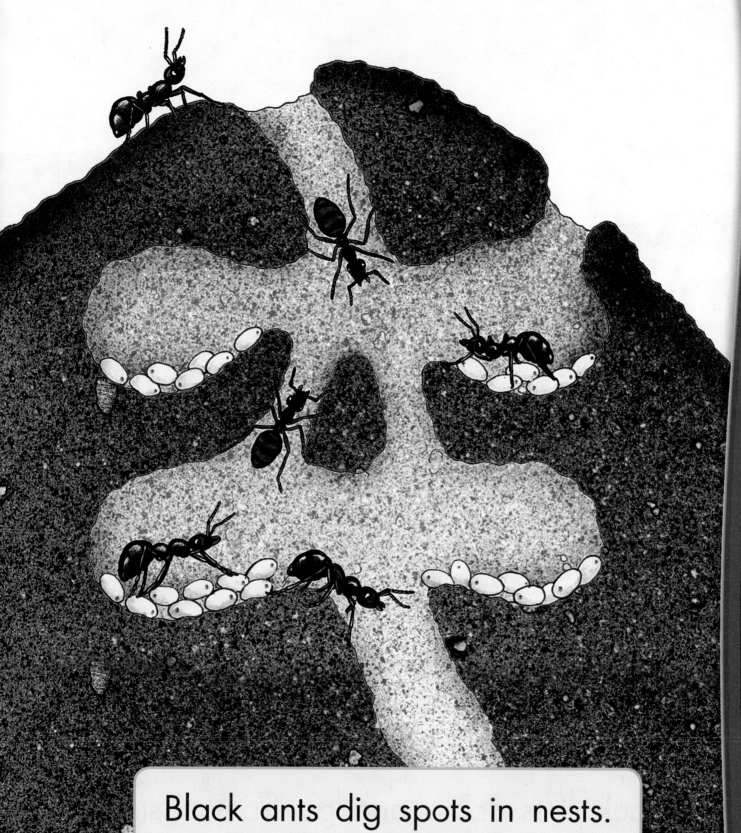

Black ants dig spots in nests.
Ants put eggs in spots.

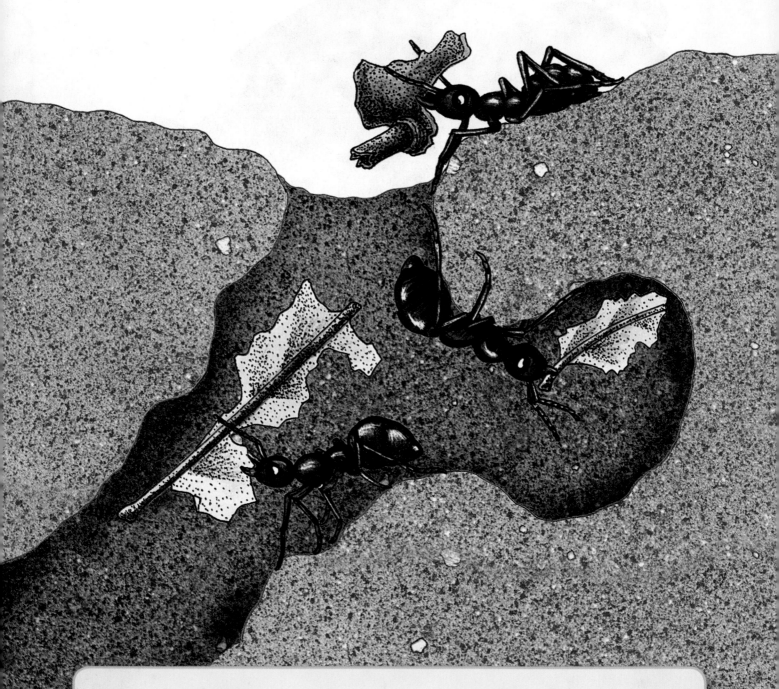

Black ants come and go from nests.
They put bug and plant bits in spots.

Ants do not like a mess in the nest.
They get rid of a big mess fast.

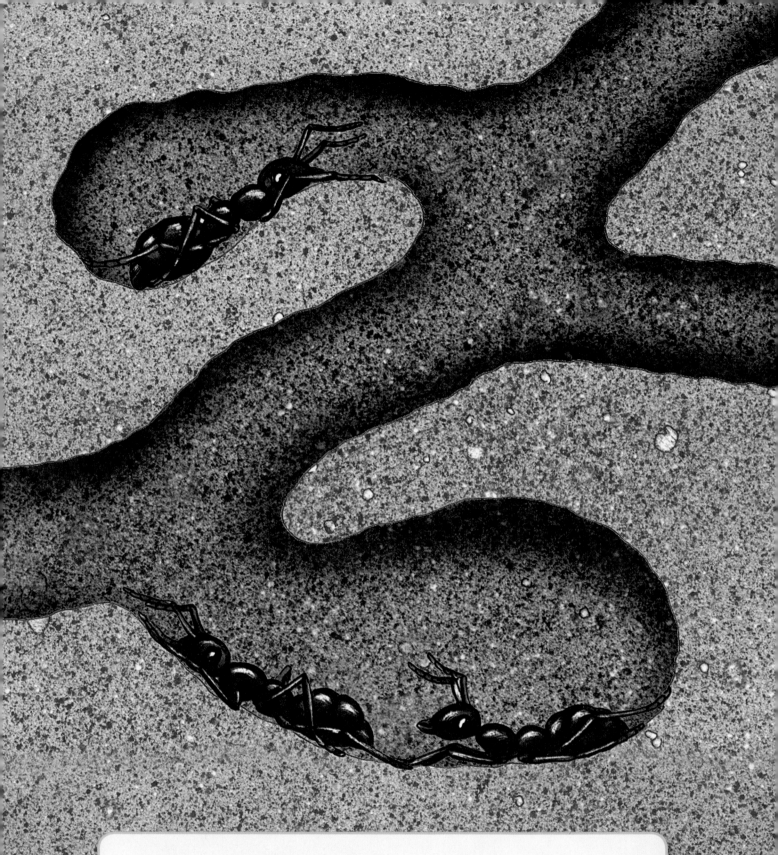

Where can black ants rest?
Black ants dig rest spots in nests.

Black ants work well together.

# Ants Must Work!

by Kim Barman ● illustrated by Gary Dunn

Drill! Drill! Drill! Drill!
Nat was drilling spots in an ant nest.

"I am sick of drilling," said Nat.
"But ants must work," said Nan.

"But not at drilling!" said Nat.
"Come! Look at ant jobs," said Nan.

Nat put his drill in its red box.
Nat and Nan ran up ten big steps.

"Ants get big plant bits," said Nan.
"I can not lift big bits," said Nat.

"Big ants help ant kids," said Nan.
"I can not stand bad kids," said Nat.

Nat ran fast.

"Where are you going?" said Nan.

"Back to drilling!" said Nat.
"Ants must work!"

# What's the Buzz?

Read Together

The queen bee runs the hive. The drone bees serve the queen.

The worker bees have different jobs. Some take care of the baby bees.

Other worker bees get nectar from flowers. They use it to make honey.

# My New Words

**come***    You can **come** to my house anytime.

**put***    When you **put** something somewhere, you set it in place.

**where***    **Where** are you going?

*tested high-frequency words

# Pictionary

work

food

# Acknowledgments

## Text

*Every effort has been made to locate the copyright owner of material reproduced in this component. Omissions brought to our attention will be corrected in subsequent editions. Grateful acknowledgment is made to the following for copyrighted material.*

**56 O'Flynn Consulting** "Welcome to Our Classroom" from *back to school* www.songs4teachers.com. Copyright © 2009 songs4teachers.com. Used by permission.

## Illustrations

**Cover:** Peter Grosshauser, Apryl Stott, Gary Dunn; **1, 4, 12–21** Peter Grosshauser; **2, 30, 33, 56** Shirley Beckes; **3, 158** Ariel Pang; **5, 22–29** Aleksey & Olga Ivanov; **7–8, 11, 160** Liz Conrad; **32–33, 50–55** Anne Kennedy; **33–40** Stacey Schuett; **58, 68–75** Sue Miller; **59–67** Apryl Stott; **59, 76–81** Victor Baldescu; **84, 98–106** Jackie Stafford; **85–90** Ashley Mims; **110, 126–133** Cathy Shimmen; **111, 134** Dan Sharp; **112–118** Drew-Brook Cormack; **136, 144–149** Alan Baker; **137, 150–157** Gary Dunn; **137–142** Lindy Burnett.

## Photographs

*Every effort has been made to secure permission and provide appropriate credit for photographic material. The publisher deeply regrets any omission and pledges to correct errors called to its attention in subsequent editions.*

*Unless otherwise acknowledged, all photographs are the property of Pearson Education, Inc.*

*Photo locators denoted as follows: Top (T), Center (C), Bottom (B), Left (L), Right (R), Background (Bkgd)*

**Cover:** (C) Blend Images/Getty Images; (CR) Comstock Images, (BR) Getty Images; **2** (BL) Getty Images; **3** (BR) Veer, Inc.; **31** (C) Brand X Pictures; **42** (BL) ©C Squared Studios/Getty Images, (TR, C, Bkgd) Getty Images; **43** (TL, C, BR) Getty Images; **44** (TR) Chas Howson/The British Museum/©DK Images, (T, C, BR, BL, Bkgd) Getty Images; **45** (C) ©Howard Davies/Corbis; **46** (TL, C, BR, BL, Bkgd) Getty Images; **47** (C) ©Henning Christoph/Das Fotarchiv/Peter Arnold, Inc.; **48** (TL, C, BL, Bkgd) Getty Images, (BR) ©MedioImages/Getty Images; **49** (C) ©Fabian Cevallos/Corbis; **57** (C) ©C Squared Studios/Getty Images; **82** (TR, CR, CL) Getty Images; **83** (C, BL) Getty Images; **85** (BR) Getty Images; **92** (C) Comstock Images; **94** (C) Getty Images; **96** (Bkgd) ©Relnhard Elsele/Corbis, (C) Getty Images; **97** (C) ©Peter Blackwell/Nature Picture Library; **108** (TR) Digital Vision, (TL, BR, BL) Getty Images, (CL) image100, (CR) ©Tim Laman/Getty Images; **109** (BL) Getty Images, (CR) ©William Smithey, Jr./Getty Images; **111** (CR) ©Robert Ross/Getty Images; **120** (C) Veer, Inc.; **121** (C) ©Robert Ross/Getty Images; **122** (C) ©blickwinkel/Hecker/Alamy; **123** (C) Getty Images; **124** (C) ©Joel Sartore/Getty Images; **135** (BR) ©Sindre Ellingsen/Alamy Images, (C) Getty Images; **159** (C) Getty Images.